THE POET'S TOOLBOX

Recess, Rhyme, and Reason

A Collection of Poems About School

Compiled and Annotated
by Patricia M. Stockland

Illustrated by
Sara Rojo Pérez

Compass Point Books
3109 West 50th Street, #115
Minneapolis, MN 55410

Visit Compass Point Books on the Internet at *www.compasspointbooks.com*
or e-mail your request to *custserv@compasspointbooks.com*

A special thank you to John, Elizabeth, and Chaneen

Permissions and Acknowledgements:
"September," 6. "September" from EVERETT ANDERSON'S YEAR by Lucille Clifton. Text Copyright © 1974 by Lucille Clifton. Reprinted by permission of Henry Holt and Company, LLC. "School Bus," 6. Copyright © 1994 by Lee Bennett Hopkins. First appeared in School Supplies, published by Simon and Schuster. Reprinted by permission of Curtis Brown, Ltd. "On the Playground," 7. Printed by permission of Patricia M. Stockland. "The 1st Day of School," 8, "The 179th Day of School," 9. "The First Day of School" and "The 179th Day of School" from LUNCH BOX MAIL AND OTHER POEMS by Jenny Whitehead. © 2001 by Jenny Whitehead. Reprinted by permission of Henry Holt and Company, LLC. "Homework," 10. Reprinted by permission of Harold Ober Associates Incorporated. Copyright © 1972, 2000 by Russell Hoban. "Swap," 11, "And the Answer Is . . .?," 12. "And the Answer Is . . .?," "Swap," from LUNCH MONEY by Carol Diggory Shields, copyright © 1995 by Carol Diggory Shields, text. Used by permission of Dutton Children's Books, an imprint of Penguin Putnam Books for Young Readers, a division of Penguin Putnam Inc. All rights reserved. "from Arithmetic," 13. Excerpt from "Arithmetic" in THE COMPLETE POEMS OF CARL SANDBURG, copyright © 1970, 1969 by Lilian Steichen Sandburg, Trustee, reprinted by permission of Harcourt, Inc. "Today," 14. TEXT COPYRIGHT © 1986 BY JEAN LITTLE. Used by permission of HarperCollins Publishers. "Yawning," 15. Reprinted by permission of Harold Ober Associates Incorporated. Copyright © 1938 by Eleanor Farjeon. "My Teacher in the Market," 16. "My Teacher in the Market" from CANTO FAMILIAR, copyright © 1995 by Gary Soto, reprinted by permission of Harcourt, Inc. "We Could Be Friends," 18. From THE WAY THINGS ARE AND OTHER POEMS by Myra Cohn Livingston. Copyright © 1974 by Myra Cohn Livingston. Used by permission of Marian Reiner. "Christopher, My Friend," 19. Every effort has been made to contact the author. Compass Point Books does not take credit for the authorship, ownership, or copyright of this poem. "Classroom," 20. Printed by permission of Patricia M. Stockland. "Some People," 21. Reprinted with the permission of Simon & Schuster Books for Young Readers, an imprint of Simon and Schuster Children's Publishing Division from POEMS by Rachel Field (Macmillan, New York, 1957). "Pencils," 22. COPYRIGHT © 1992 BY BARBARA JUSTER ESBENSEN. Used by permission of HarperCollins Publishers. "The Poet Pencil," 23. "The Poet Pencil" by Jesús Carlos Soto Morfín; translated by Judith Infante from THE TREE IS OLDER THAN YOU ARE, selected by Naomi Shihab Nye, Aladdin Paperbacks/Simon & Schuster Children's Publishing Division, 1998. "Mixed-Up School," 24. Copyright © 1975 by X. J. Kennedy. First appeared in One Winter Night In August, published by Scribner. Reprinted by permission of Curtis Brown, Ltd. "Country School," 25. From OFFICIAL ENTRY BLANK, University of Nebraska Press, 1969. Reprinted by permission of the author.

Content Advisers: Jane K. Volkman, Patricia Kirkpatrick, Ph.D.
Rights Researcher: Nancy Loewen
Designer: The Design Lab

Library of Congress Cataloging-in-Publication Data
Recess, rhyme, and reason : a collection of poems about school / compiled and annotated
by Patricia M. Stockland.
    p. cm. — (The poet's toolbox)
Summary: An anthology of poems about school, plus "Toolbox tips" that help the reader
understand poetry and how poems are written.
ISBN 0-7565-0564-X (hardcover)
1. Schools—Juvenile poetry. 2. Education—Juvenile poetry.
3. School children—Juvenile poetry. 4. Children's poetry, American.
(1. Schools—Poetry. 2. Education—Poetry. 3. American poetry.)
I. Stockland, Patricia M. II. Title. III. Series.
PS595.S34R43 2004
808.81'93557—dc22   2003017105

Table of Contents

NOTE: In this book, words that are defined in the glossary are in **bold** the first time they appear in the text.

Open Your Toolbox

Every day at school, you do a hundred different things. Some parts of school are boring, but admit it: there are times when you're excited and fascinated at school. How do you tell someone about those moments—when you suddenly discover you love reading a new kind of book, or you meet a friend you'll keep for life, or when everyone at your lunch table makes you so angry you just want to walk away? Poetry can be a way to describe those things—recess, friends, books, teachers, math, reading, writing, the school bus . . . anything!

WHAT DOES POETRY DO?

Poetry helps energize your imagination. Poetry plays with words in ways you never imagined. Ordinary words become suddenly mysterious or exciting. Poetry opens your ears to different sounds—sentences can play like music. Everyone has smart ideas, and poetry can be a new language with which to share those ideas.

DOES A POET USE A TOOLBOX?

Poets use many different tools and materials to build their poems. The stuff that happens to poets every day can become material for a poem. Poets' tools include parts of speech (such as nouns, verbs, and adjectives), ways of writing (like different forms or types of poetry), and the interesting sounds that letters and words make when they're combined (like rhymes and repeated letters). This book will show you some of the tools that poets use to create poems, and it might even help you to write some of your own poetry!

HOW DOES THE POET'S TOOLBOX WORK?

First, read all the poems—they are all about different parts of school. After you read each one, take a look at the Toolbox Tip on the bottom of the page. These Toolbox Tips will help you to understand a poetry tool the writer has used, or they might give you a hint about where the poet found the idea for that poem. Near the back of the book, you'll have the chance to begin using these tools yourself!

September

I already know where Africa is
and I already know how to
count to ten and
I went to school every day last year,
why do I have to go again?

—Lucille Clifton

School Bus

This wide-awake
freshly-painted-yellow
school bus

readied for Fall

carries us all—

    Sixteen boys—
    Fourteen girls—

    Thirty pairs of sleepy eyes

and

hundreds
upon
hundreds

of

school supplies.

—Lee Bennett Hopkins

MAKE BELIEVE
When poets give human traits, or characteristics, to something that isn't human, they are using **personification.** It grabs your attention by describing that thing in a new way. Can a school bus really be wide-awake?

On the Playground

All   ease . . .
   the   great
      swings   with
           move

I
wish
a
swing
were
left
for
me.

—Patricia M. Stockland

Listen . . . What do you see?

LISTEN . . . WHAT DO YOU SEE?

TOOLBOX TIP In a **concrete** poem, words are arranged to make a shape. The shape they make usually relates to what the poem is about. What shapes do the words on this page make?

The 1st Day of School

Brand-new crayons and
   unchipped chalk.
Brand-new haircut,
   spotless smock.
Brand-new rules—
   "No running, please."
Brand-new pair of
   nervous knees.
Brand-new faces,
   unclogged glue.
Brand-new hamster,
   shiny shoes.
Brand-new teacher,
   classroom fun.
Brand-new school year's
   just begun.

—Jenny Whitehead

TOOLBOX TIP

SOUNDS THE SAME

When words end in the same sound, they **rhyme.** "Fun" and "begun" rhyme, but imperfect rhymes like "chalk" and "smock" work, too. These are called slant rhymes. Can you find other pairs of rhymes in these poems?

8

The 179th Day of School

Broken crayons and
    mop-head hair.
Scuffed-up shoes and
    squeaky chair.
Dried-up paste,
    chewed, leaky pens.
Dusty chalkboard,
    lifelong friends.
One inch taller,
    bigger brain.
Well-worn books,
    old grape-juice stain.
Paper airplanes,
    classroom cheer.
School is done and
    summer's here!

—Jenny Whitehead

Mirror images

 TOOLBOX TIP   **MIRROR IMAGES**
These poems mirror each other. The second poem repeats ideas from the first, but in a different way. This allows the poet to **compare and contrast** the two days. What's different about the 179th day of school?

9

Homework

Homework sits on top of Sunday, squashing Sunday flat.
Homework has the smell of Monday, homework's very fat.
Heavy books and piles of paper, answers I don't know.
Sunday evening's almost finished, now I'm going to go
Do my homework in the kitchen. Maybe just a snack,
Then I'll sit right down and start as soon as I run back
For some chocolate sandwich cookies. Then I'll really do
All that homework in a minute. First I'll see what new
Show they've got on television in the living room.
Everybody's laughing there, but misery and gloom
And a full refrigerator are where I am at.
I'll just have another sandwich. Homework's very fat.

—Russell Hoban

CATCHY BEAT
TOOLBOX TIP **Rhythm** is the beat in poetry that sometimes makes it feel like music. It can be created by rhymes or syllables. You can measure rhythm in **meter**—just count the stressed syllables, or beats, in each line. How many beats are in each line of this poem?

Swap

Mom made me a peanut butter sandwich,
I traded at lunch for a tuna on rye.
Swapped my orange for Jonathan's corn chips,
And traded my cookies for a marshmallow pie.

Traded the chips for a handful of pretzels,
Gave up my milk for a tropical punch.
Changed the tuna for Ben's bologna,
Swapped the pie for the cake in Kim's lunch.

Gave the bologna for a bagel with cream cheese,
Swapped the cake for yummy Gummy Bears.
Sold the punch for a shiny, new quarter,
Traded the pretzels for a nice, ripe pear.

Bought some cold milk with the quarter,
Traded the bears for a pudding cup.
Swapped the bagel for Joe's ham sandwich,
Exchanged the pudding for a Fruit Roll-Up.

Gave the ham for a peanut butter sandwich,
Took an orange for the fruit roll snack.
Swapped the pear for two chocolate-chip cookies . . .
I think I just got my old lunch back.

—Carol Diggory Shields

TOOLBOX TIP

SEE A PATTERN?

A **pattern** can happen in a poem when the poet pairs up
lines that rhyme. Can you figure out this poet's rhyming
pattern? Where do the rhyming words fall in the lines?

And the Answer Is . . . . ?

Teacher, please don't look at me—
The answer is a mystery.
I'm staring into empty air,
I'm sliding underneath my chair.
I'm making myself very small,
I wish I wasn't here at all.
Teacher, teacher, pass me by,
Please pick on some other guy.

Teacher, teacher, call on me—
I know the answer, can't you see?
This one's a wrap, a snap, a breeze.
Just look in my direction, please!
I'm almost bouncing off my chair,
I'm waving both hands in the air.
Teacher, teacher, ask me first,
'Cause if you don't I think I'll burst.

—Carol Diggory Shields

Who is it?

TOOLBOX TIP

WHO IS IT?

Within a single poem, a poet can take on the **voice** of many characters, or one character in different moods. Do you think the two parts of this poem are about the same person or two different students?

from Arithmetic

Arithmetic is where numbers fly
    like pigeons in and out of your head.
Arithmetic tells you how many you lose or win
    if you know how many you had
    before you lost or won.
Arithmetic is seven eleven all good children
    go to heaven---or five six bundle of sticks.
Arithmetic is numbers you squeeze from your
    head to your hand to your pencil to your paper
    till you get the right answer . . .
If you have two animal crackers, one good and one bad,
    and you eat one and a striped zebra
    with streaks all over him eats the other,
    how many animal crackers will you have
    if somebody offers you five six seven and you say
    No no no and you say Nay nay nay
    and you say Nix nix nix?
If you ask your mother for one fried egg
    for breakfast and she gives you
    two fried eggs and you eat
    both of them, who is better in arithmetic,
    you or your mother?

—Carl Sandburg

TOOLBOX TIP

NONSENSE

Poems don't have to make sense . . . to make sense!
Read this poem once and it sounds like nonsense.
Read it again . . . does it start making sense?

Today

Today I will not live up to my potential.
Today I will not relate well to my peer group.
Today I will not contribute in class.
   I will not volunteer one thing.
Today I will not strive to do better.
Today I will not achieve or adjust or grow enriched
   or get involved.
I will not put up my hand even if the teacher is wrong
   and I can prove it.

Today I might eat the eraser off my pencil.
I'll look at clouds.
I'll be late.
I don't think I'll wash.

I need a rest.

—Jean Little

No tool?

TOOLBOX TIP

NO TOOL?
This poem is written in **free verse**—it doesn't use any
rhymes or patterns. Instead, it repeats words. Does free verse
help show the bad mood of the speaker in the poem?

Yawning

Sometimes—I'm sorry—but sometimes,
Sometimes, yes, sometimes I'm bored.
It may be because I'm an idiot;
It may be because I'm floored;

It may be because it is raining,
It may be because it is hot,
It may be because I have eaten
Too much, or because I have not.

But sometimes I *cannot* help yawning
(I'm sorry!) the whole morning through—
And when Teacher's turning her back on us,
It may be that she's yawning too.

—Eleanor Farjeon

Repeat, repeat, repeat

TOOLBOX TIP

REPEAT, REPEAT, REPEAT
Sometimes, a good way to make your point is to repeat it and repeat
it. And repeat it! **Repetition** helps others remember your point.
Do the repeated words in these poems help make any points?

My Teacher in the Market

Who would suppose
On a Saturday
That my teacher
Would balance
Tomatoes in her hands
And sniff them
Right under my nose.
I'm María,
The girl with a Band-Aid
On each knee,
Pink scars the shape
Of check marks
On homework.
I'm hiding by the bags
Of potatoes,
Tiptoeing and curious.
I've never seen
My teacher in jeans
And a T-shirt,
And tennies with a hole
Where the little
Toe rubs. She
Bags the tomatoes

And a pinch of chiles.
She presses a thumb
Gently into ripe avocados,
Three for a dollar
Because they're black,
Black, but pretty black.
I wave to my teacher
And then duck,
Giggling. I look up.
She lifts a watermelon
Into her arms,
Melon with its army
Of seeds to spit
Across a sidewalk.
I can't imagine *her* doing *that,*
My teacher, my teacher.
She weighs nectarines
And plums, peaches
With their belly
Of itchy fur.
I wave again,
And duck. It's funny
Seeing my teacher

Drop a grape
Into her mouth,
Same mouth that says
4 times 6 is 36,
I mean 24. She lowers
The bunch of grapes
Into a plastic bag.
Then she turns
Toward the potatoes
And finds me peeking through.
When she says,
"Oh, it's María,
My little potato eyes,"
I blush and squint my eyes shut.
When I open them,
She's gone,
Her shopping cart
Now swinging
Down the aisle
Of cereals,
Leaving me,
María, little potato eyes.

—Gary Soto

WORDS MAKE PICTURES

TOOLBOX TIP

Imagery is the picture you get in your mind when you read a poem.
Details like sounds, smells, colors, and tastes can help create that picture.
How many different foods, actions, and colors does this poet show you?

We Could Be Friends

We could be friends
Like friends are supposed to be.
You, picking up the telephone
Calling me

to come over and play
or take a walk,
finding a place
to sit and talk,

Or just goof around
Like friends do,
Me, picking up the telephone
Calling you.

—Myra Cohn Livingston

TOOLBOX TIP

FRIENDS TO THE END . . .
School is a great place to make friends—and friends can be a great topic for poetry because we know so much about them. What kinds of things come to mind when you think about your friends?

Christopher, my friend

Freckles all over,
Ginger hair but very kind,
Christopher my friend.

—James Baker

TOOLBOX TIP

HAIKU FOR YOU

Haikus are short poems. They usually have 17 beats—
five in the first and last lines and seven in the middle. James
Baker was only 10 years old when he wrote this one!

Children
Learning and laughing
And
Singing
Smiling
Reading and writing
Or adding and subtracting
Or making
Memories

—Patricia M. Stockland

TOOLBOX TIP

READING IN ANOTHER DIRECTION . . .

An **acrostic** poem goes in more than one direction! If you put the first letter of each line together, it will spell a word. Sometimes the word is the title or main idea of the poem. What do you think the poet was writing about?

Some People

Isn't it strange some people make
You feel so tired inside,
Your thoughts begin to shrivel up
Like leaves all brown and dried!

But when you're with some other ones,
It's stranger still to find
Your thoughts as thick as fireflies
All shiny in your mind!

—Rachel Field

TOOLBOX TIP

STOPPING TO THINK

Sometimes poets separate ideas with **stanzas.** These are groups of lines
in poetry that act like paragraphs. Here, the poet begins a new thought
after skipping a line. Meeting new people might make you stop to think.

Pencils

The rooms in a pencil
are narrow
but elephants   castles and watermelons
fit in

In a pencil
noisy words yell for attention
and quiet words wait their turn

How did they slip
into such a tight place?
Who
gives them their
lunch?

From a broken pencil
an unbroken poem will come!
There is a long story living
in even the shortest pencil

Every word in your
pencil
is fearless   ready to walk
the blue tightrope lines
Ready
to teeter and smile
down   Ready to come right out
and show you
thinking!

—Barbara Esbensen

TOOLBOX TIP

WHAT'S IN THERE?
When poets give the qualities of one thing to something else, they are using
metaphors. The metaphors of a room and a river suggest what might be inside your
pencil. Although pencils don't really have rooms or rivers, what could these poets mean?

The Poet Pencil

Once upon a time a pencil wanted to write poetry but it didn't have a point. One day a boy put it into the sharpener, and in place of a point, a river appeared.

— Jesús Carlos Soto Morfín

Translated by Judith Infante from Spanish

TOOLBOX TIP

TWICE AS NICE
People all over the world write poetry. Sometimes these poems are **translated.** A person will write the same poem in another language so even more people can enjoy it.

Mixed-Up School

We have a crazy mixed-up school.
Our teacher Mrs. Cheetah
Makes us talk backwards. Nicer cat
You wouldn't want to meet a.

To start the day we eat our lunch,
Then do some heavy dome-work.
The boys' and girls' rooms go to us,
The hamster marks our homework.

At recess time we race inside
To put on diving goggles,
Play pin-the-donkey-on-the-tail,
Ball-foot or ap-for-bobbles.

Old Cheetah, with a chunk of chalk,
Writes right across two blackbirds,
And when she says, "Go home!" we walk
The whole way barefoot backwards.

—X. J. Kennedy

Meter reader

METER READER

TOOLBOX TIP

You can read the rhythm in this poem—all of the lines
have either seven or eight beats. Which lines have seven?
Which have eight? Is there a pattern to the meter?

Country School

The Apple Valley School has closed its books,
wiped off its blackboard, put away its chalk;
the valley children with their parents' looks
ride buses down the road their parents walked.

The Apple Valley School is full of bales,
and the bell was auctioned off a year ago.
Under the teeter-totter, spotted quail
have nested where the grass would never grow.

The well is dry where boys caught garter snakes
and chased the girls into their memories.
High on the hill, nobody climbs to shake
the few ripe apples from the broken tree.

—Ted Kooser

TOOLBOX TIP

WHERE ARE YOU FROM?
Ted Kooser was born and raised in the Midwest,
where a lot of farming takes place. Do you think
this setting helped him write this poem?

THE POET'S TOOLBOX

Collect Your Tools

Poets use a lot of tools to build their poems. These tools help to create different types of poems, like rhyming poems, free verse poems, acrostic poems, concrete poems, and even haikus. What poetry tools have you learned? When you find the answers to the questions on these pages, you're learning to work just like a poet. (Hint: Need help with a word you don't understand? Look in The Poet's Toolbox Glossary on page 28.)

1. When words end in the same sound, they **rhyme,** such as the poem "The 1st Day of School" on page 8. Find other poems that have rhyming lines. Do the rhymes always appear in the same **pattern?**

2. On page 10, you read "Homework," a poem that has 13 beats in each line. The number of beats and the way they are played is **rhythm.** Can you find other poems that have the same number of beats in each of their lines?

3. Jean Little repeats the phrase "Today I will not" a lot in her poem (page 14). Find other poems that use the tool of **repetition.**

4. On pages 8 and 9, Jenny Whitehead wrote about the first day of school and the last day of school. Poets often use this tool—**comparing and contrasting** things that are similar and things that are different. Do other poems in this book use the compare-and-contrast tool?

5. "Today" (page 14) is a **free verse** poem—it doesn't use rhyming words or stick to set patterns. The poem sounds like someone is just talking. These things make free verse poems different from rhyming poems. Find another free verse poem in this book.

Congratulations! Now you know a whole lot more about the tools poets use, and you're probably able to use some of these tools yourself. You've seen lots of examples. Now go to the next page, and get out your pencil and paper. It's time to build your own poems!

You know how to use some poetry tools, so it's time to go to work. Here's an activity that will help you get going on writing some of your own poems.

Keeping a Journal

Ideas for poems are all around you every day, but if you don't write these ideas right away, you'll forget them quickly. Keeping a journal is easy and fun, and you might wind up doing it the rest of your life.

1. Get a new notebook, something small that you can carry all the time. It can be a plain notebook, nothing fancy.

2. Once a day, sit down to write in your journal. You might find it easy to remember to write in your journal if you decide to do it at the same time every day.

3. What goes in your journal? *Anything!* Write down whatever grabbed your attention that day. For instance, here are some things you can write in your journal:

- **People . . .** other kids at school, your teachers, your principal, your parents, your brothers and sisters. Or, how about the president of the United States, your favorite athlete or pop singer . . . or yourself!

- **Places . . .** the ordinary places you go every day (school, the grocery store, your best friend's house), or on special occasions (restaurants, parties, vacations), or the town you live in and the cities you visit . . .anywhere!

- **Things . . .** books you've read, movies you watch, clothes you wear, foods, toys . . . anything!

- **Dreams . . .** keep your journal by your bed and write down your dreams as soon as you wake up.

- **Your senses—*all of them* . . .** In addition to writing what you saw today, how about what you smelled? Heard? Touched? Tasted?

4. Having trouble getting started? The first few days, just write down one journal entry. Keep it simple–don't write too much, just a couple of sentences. After a few days, write three entries a day. Keep adding more as the days pass.

Now, become a poet. After a week of keeping a journal, read back over what you've written. Choose one entry that you really like, an entry that shows you something you can really see clearly. Then look at the poet's tools you practiced on the previous page. Try using some of those tools to turn your journal entry into a poem. For example, you could write an acrostic poem like the one on page 20, or repeat words like the poem on page 14. Go to work!

Go to Work

The Poet's Toolbox Glossary can help you understand poetry tools used in this book and others in this series. Words in **color** are tools found in this book. Words in **black** are other poetry tools that will also be helpful as you work on your own poetry.

Acrostic poems use the first letters of each line to spell out a word or name.

Alliteration (ah-LIT-er-A-shun) is a tool that helps with sounds. It repeats consonant sounds or vowel sounds that are the same, like the "m" in "marvelous malted milk" or the "o" sound in "Go home, Joe."

Comparing and contrasting helps you to see what is the same or different about two or more ideas, objects, people, places, or anything. For example, a poet might compare an old shoe to a new shoe by listing the way the two shoes smell (stinky or fresh), look (dirty or clean), and feel (comfortable or stiff).

Concrete poems look like something you can touch. The way words and lines are arranged on the page is just as important as what they mean. A poem about the sun might be round like the sun, or a poem about a swing might look like the words are swinging.

Couplets are pairs of rhyming lines that usually have the same number of beats. Couplets make their own point, create a separate image, or summarize the idea of a poem.

Free verse poetry is poetry that doesn't have to rhyme or stay in stanzas, or even lines. Don't let the word "free" trick you, though. The poet might use other tools to keep the poem tied together, like repeating the same sounds or words.

Haiku usually has 17 syllables (or beats) in three lines—five syllables in the first and last lines and seven in the middle. A haiku is a short poem, usually about nature and the seasons.

Imagery is what you picture in your mind when you read a poem. Details like colors, sounds, sizes, shapes, comparisons, smells, and flavors all help create imagery.

Limericks are humorous poems with five lines. The last words of the first, second, and third lines rhyme, as do the last words of the shorter third and fourth lines. The shorter lines have two stressed beats, and the longer lines have three stressed beats.

Metaphors show how two different things are similar by calling one thing something else, such as if you call clouds "balls of cotton."

Meter measures the number of syllables, or beats, in each line of a poem. If you can count the beats, you can determine the meter. For example, some types of poems always have 10 beats per line. Others have 12.

Onomatopoeia (ON-o-MA-tow-PEE-ya) is another cool word tool poets use. This is when the word suggests the sound or action it means, like "buzz," "hiss," and "boom."

Patterns are several things that are repeated in the same way several times. Many poems create a pattern by repeating rhyming words at the end of each line.

Personification gives human characteristics, or traits, to something that isn't human. It makes an object or animal seem human or come to life.

Repetition is what happens when poets repeat certain words, phrases, or sounds. Repetition can help create patterns. It can also help make or emphasize a point.

Rhymes are words that end in the same sound. For example, "clock" rhymes with "dock." Rhyming sounds don't have to be spelled the same way. "Pest" rhymes with "dressed."

Rhythm is the beat you can feel in poetry, like a tempo in music. Syllables, or beats, help create rhythm. Rhymes can create rhythm, too. You can measure rhythm through meter.

Similes are comparisons using "as" or "like." When you use a simile, you are saying that one thing is similar to another. Similes can help you create personification. They are also a lot like metaphors.

Stanzas are like paragraphs for poetry. They are groups of lines that sit together and are usually separated by a blank line. Sometimes a poet begins a new thought in a new stanza.

Structure is how a poem was built. A poet can build a poem using lines and stanzas.

Synonyms are words that mean almost the same thing.

Translated means the poem was originally written in a different language.

Voice is the speaker in a poem. It can be one person, or a bunch of different people. It can be animals, objects, or even the poet.

AT THE LIBRARY

Alarcón, Francisco X. Illustrated by Maya Christina Gonzalez. *From the Bellybutton of the Moon and Other Summer Poems.* San Francisco: Children's Book Press, 1998.

Hughes, Langston. Illustrated by Brian Pinkney. *The Dream Keeper and Other Poems.* New York: Knopf, 1994.

Kennedy, X.J. Illustrated by Joy Allen. *Exploding Gravy: Poems to Make You Laugh.* Boston: Little, Brown, 2002.

Lansky, Bruce. Illustrated by Stephen Carpenter. *If Pigs Could Fly—And Other Deep Thoughts: A Collection of Funny Poems.* Minnetonka, Minn.: Meadowbrook Press, 2000.

Shapiro, Karen Jo. Illustrated by Matt Faulkner. *Because I Could Not Stop My Bike, and Other Poems.* Watertown, Mass.: Whispering Coyote, 2003.

Silverstein, Shel. *Falling Up: Poems and Drawings.* New York: HarperCollins, 1996.

Wong, Janet S. *A Suitcase of Seaweed, and Other Poems.* New York: Margaret K. McElderry Books, 1996.

Finding More Poetry

ON THE ROAD

Riley Museum

528 Lockerbie St.

Indianapolis, IN 46202

317/631-5885

To visit the historical Victorian home of poet

James Whitcomb Riley

WEB SITES

For more information on **poetry,** use FactHound
to track down Web sites related to this book.

1. Go to *www.compasspointbooks.com/facthound*

2. Type in this book ID: **075650564X**

3. Click on the FETCH IT button.

Your trusty FactHound will fetch the best Web sites for you!

ABOUT THE AUTHOR

Patricia M. Stockland has a Bachelor of Arts degree in English from South Dakota State University. She lives in Minnesota and is currently completing her Master of Arts thesis in literature from Minnesota State University, Mankato. She has taught composition and enjoys both writing and helping others write. Patricia is an editor and author of children's nonfiction books.

ABOUT THE ILLUSTRATOR

Sara Rojo Pérez was born in Madrid and now lives in Cádiz on the southern coast of Spain. For many years she worked as the creative director of an animation studio, creating both films and advertisements. Sara works in many different media—from paint in oils or acrylics to computer illustration to sculptures and tapestries. In addition to her artwork, Sara enjoys horseback riding and reading fantasy and mystery novels.

INDEX